P9-BZT-218

J
636.7
STO

EYE TO EYE WITH DOGS

DACHSHUNDS

Lynn M. Stone

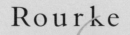

Rourke

Publishing LLC

Vero Beach, Florida 32964

© 2003 Rourke Publishing LLC

All rights reserved. No part of this book may be reproduced or utilized in any form or by any means, electronic or mechanical including photocopying, recording, or by any information storage and retrieval system without permission in writing from the publisher.

www.rourkepublishing.com

PHOTO CREDITS: All photos © Lynn M. Stone

Cover: *The first dachshunds were hounds used to follow game animals. They were brought from Germany about 500 years ago.*

Acknowledgments: For their help in the preparation of this book, the author thanks humans Cheryl and George Rausch of Cherylin Dachshunds (North Winamac, IN) and several of their cooperative canines.

Editor: Frank Sloan

Cover and page design by Nicola Stratford

Library of Congress Cataloging-in-Publication Data

Stone, Lynn M.
    Dachshunds / Lynn M. Stone
        p. cm — (Eye to eye with dogs)
    Summary: A brief introduction to the physical characteristics, temperament, uses, and breeding history of the dachshund.
    Includes bibliographical references (p.).
    ISBN 1-58952-326-1
    1. Dachshunds—Juvenile literature. [1. Dachshunds. 2. Dogs.] I. Title.

SF429.D25 S76 2002
636.753'8—dc21   212002017841

Printed in the USA

MP/W

Table of Contents

The shorthaired dachshund shows the long, lean body of the breed.

The Dachshund

The dachshund (DOCKS hoond) is the original "wiener" dog. It has a long, frankfurter-like body, deep chest, and short legs.

The original **ancestor** of all dogs was the wolf. But people have been choosing the parents of pups for more than 12,000 years.

STANDARD DACHSHUND FACTS	
Weight:	11-32 pounds (5-14.5 kilograms)
Height:	8-9 inches (21-23 centimeters)
Country of Origin:	Germany
Life Span:	12-14 years

By choosing carefully, human dog **breeders** developed many kinds, or **breeds**, of dogs. Some breeds, like the dachshund, aren't even shaped like wolves!

Dachshunds look very little like the wolf, the original ancestor of dogs.

Dachshunds were developed to slip into narrow places.

Most dog breeds were developed for people's special uses. The dachshund, for example, was developed as a hunter of burrowing animals. What better dog than the long, frankfurter-like dachshund to slip into a rabbit or badger burrow?

Dachshunds are rarely used as hunting dogs today in North America. They are popular, though, as home companions. Among **purebred** dogs, they ranked fourth in American Kennel Club (AKC) **registrations** in 2001. They narrowly missed being among the top ten breeds in Canada.

Dachshunds are one of the most popular purebred dog breeds in North America.

Dachshunds' hound and terrier background made them brave hunters.

Dachshunds of the Past

The first dachshund-type dogs showed up in Germany at least 500 years ago. Their name, which is German, means "badger dog."

The dachshunds' early dog ancestors were hounds. Hounds were used to follow game animals. Hounds led breeders to develop fearless, **aggressive** terriers. Terriers were used to chase and kill **game**. Often they would enter the den of the animal they chased.

Some dog experts group dachshunds with hounds. Others put them with terriers. The dachshund's job was to chase, corner, and attack game animals. Small dachshunds were used to hunt rabbits. Larger sizes hunted other prey, such as foxes.

North American dachshunds are raised for companionship and show competition rather than for hunting.

Smooth-coated dachshunds (left) were developed before the wirehaired variety (right).

In the late 1800s, breeders began to **mate** shiny, smooth-coated dachshunds with other small breeds. They included pinschers, terriers, schnauzers, and spaniels. This led to the development of longhaired and wirehaired dachshunds.

The American Kennel Club (AKC) recognizes two sizes of dachshunds: the standard and the miniature. In Germany, dachshunds come in three sizes. Each size class is based on the dog's chest size. Some German dachshunds are still worked. The dog's chest size determines how small a burrow it can enter.

MINIATURE DACHSHUND FACTS

Weight: 9-10 pounds (4-5 kilograms)
Height: 5-6 inches (13-15.5 centimeters)
Country of Origin: Germany
Life Span: 12-14 years

The miniature dachshund (shown here) is the smaller of two dachshund sizes recognized by the American Kennel Club.

Curiosity leads a smooth-coated dachshund into—and out of—a basket.

Looks

Dachshund owners have a wide choice of types. There are different sizes, coats, and even shapes. American dachshunds raised for dog shows, for example, have deeper chests and shorter legs than dachshunds in Germany.

All dachshunds have fairly long, sharp **muzzles** and floppy ears. But their heads look quite different. The wirehaired has a bushy face, like a schnauzer's. The longhaired dachshund's face looks much like a spaniel's.

Dachshund Companions

Dachshunds are usually fine family companions. They are bold, curious, and playful. And because they are small, they make happy lap dogs.

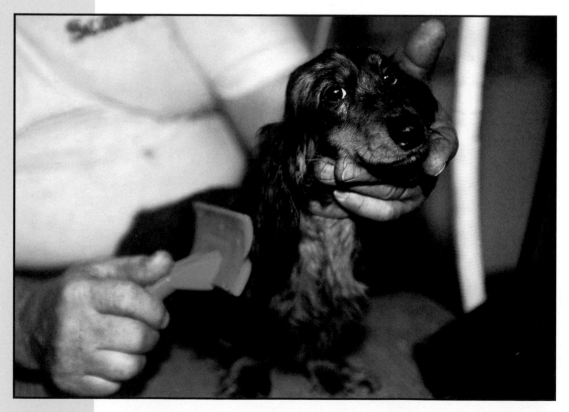

A wirehaired miniature dachshund gets a grooming from its owner.

Wirehaired dachshunds tend to be more outgoing than other types of the breed.

Dachshunds are comfortable with children they know. Some, however, may snap at strangers.

Dachshunds do well in small homes and yards. But like their ancestors, they still enjoy hunting, even as a "hobby." They hunt by following a scent.

Dachshunds can be yippy. Their barking makes them good watchdogs, but barking doesn't always please their human companions.

Longhaired dachshunds are usually more quiet and less terrier-like than other dachshunds. Wirehairs are often more outgoing than other dachshunds.

The laid-back longhaired dachshund has a head like a spaniel.

A Note About Dogs

Puppies are cute and cuddly, but buying one should never be done without serious thought. Choosing the right breed of dog requires some homework. And remember that a dog will require more than love and great patience. It will require food, exercise, grooming, a warm, safe place to live, and medical care.

A dog can be your best friend, but you need to be its best friend, too. For more information about buying and owning a dog, contact the American Kennel Club at http://www.akc.org/index.cfm or the Canadian Kennel Club at http://www.ckc.ca/.

Glossary

aggressive (uh GRES iv) — to act forcefully

ancestor (AN ses tur) — one in the past from whom an animal has descended; direct relative from the past

breeders (BREE duhrz) — people who raise animals, such as dogs, and carefully choose the mothers and fathers for more dogs

breeds (BREEDZ) — particular kinds of domestic animals within a larger group, such as the dachshund breed within the dog group

game (GAYM) — any animal that can be hunted within the law

mate (MAYT) — to pair with another dog for the purpose of having pups

muzzles (MUZ uhlz) — the nose and jaws of animals; the snouts

purebred (PYOOR bred) — an animal of a single (pure) breed

registrations (rehj uh STRAY shunz) — official records of membership in a group

Index

Further Reading

Wilcox, Charlotte: *The Dachshund*. Capstone, 2001

Websites to Visit

Dachshund Club of America at http://www.dachshund-dca.org/
The Dachshund Network at http://www.thedachshundnetwork.com
The Dog Owner's Guide – Dachshunds at
http://www.canismajor.com/dog/dachs.html

About the Author

Lynn Stone is the author of over 400 children's books. He is a talented
natural history photographer as well. Lynn, a former teacher, travels
worldwide to photograph wildlife in its natural habitat.